Original title:
Tassels of Time

Copyright © 2025 Creative Arts Management OÜ
All rights reserved.

Author: Robert Ashford
ISBN HARDBACK: 978-1-80586-188-1
ISBN PAPERBACK: 978-1-80586-660-2

The Stitches of Now

In the fabric of days, we all seem to thread,
Slicing moments like cheese, with a grin and a spread.
Time takes a leap, then trips on its lace,
Stitching up laughs, in a wild, wobbly race.

The clock strikes a joke, but it's never on time,
Tickling the seconds, with a rhythm and rhyme.
We patch up our worries with colorful thread,
Dancing with shadows, till the fun's fully spread.

A needle of laughter, pulling seams so tight,
Ripping through silence, transforming the night.
Frolicking futures, like bubbles that pop,
Catch them while laughing, before they all drop.

With joy as our fabric, we'll stretch and we'll bend,
Crafting the quirky, each stitch just a friend.
So let's skip along, through this wacky old cloth,
Where the stitches of now make us chuckle and froth.

Weaving the Past

In grandma's trunk, a treasure lies,
Old socks and ties, what a surprise!
A tapestry of laughter threads,
Each stitch a tale of silly spreads.

A hat from Uncle Joe's bold phase,
With feathers bright, a fashion craze.
Mom finds her bell-bottomed jeans,
And bursts out laughing at old routines.

Whispers of the Hourglass

The sands slip down, a quirky jest,
On each grain, a meme to test.
A wink, a nod, a tickly prank,
As clocks do dance, in silly rank.

A minute's rue, a second's rave,
A calendar's a messy knave.
It holds our goals, yet steps aside,
And laughs as we take each wild ride.

Fragments of Revelation

Each photo's snap, a bit askew,
The birthday cake, a dog in blue.
Great Aunt Ethel with a crown,
What were we thinking, upside down?

The past is full of goofy sights,
Of silly wigs and wobbly lights.
With every frame, a chuckle's found,
Revealing joy where laughs abound.

Echoes Beneath the Clock

Tick-tock goes the wall's old friend,
A jester's laugh, it seems to send.
As time unfolds with playful grace,
It gives us time to smile and chase.

A minute here, a second there,
Turns out, life's one big affair.
With winks and quirks through all these chimes,
Echoes tease us with clever rhymes.

Timelines Intertwined

In a world where clocks can't tick,
A toaster runs on cosmic trick.
Yesterday and tomorrow collide,
As squirrels steal minutes, they slide.

Jellybeans bounce from one year to next,
Time's a prankster, never perplexed.
With a wink, it pulls the string,
And laughter's the song that it sings.

Hours of Wandering

Why does time skip, hop, and dance?
It's wearing mismatched socks by chance.
Each hour is like a wobbly bike,
Riding through history, what a hike!

Naps are treasures, snatched away,
As minutes giggle, frolic, and play.
A game of hide and seek, oh dear!
I've lost my sense of time, I fear!

The Weavers of Destiny

Weaving roads like spaghetti strands,
With tangled paths and joker hands.
The weavers chuckle, slip and slide,
In their vibrant hats, they confide.

With each thread pulled, giggles ignite,
Turning blunders into delight.
For every knot and twist they sow,
Is a tale that tickles, oh what a show!

Tales in the Tapestry

In a tapestry where stories meld,
Mice wear capes while cheese is held.
Days are buttons, nights are threads,
That patch together the thoughts in heads.

Frogs leap from patterns, quite absurd,
Singing songs that sound like herds.
The yarns of giggles twist and shout,
As we unravel life, no doubt!

The Loom of Yesterday

In a web of wobbly thread,
I spun my hopes and dreams instead.
Mocking clocks and silly chimes,
Tick-tock antics blur the lines.

The yarn is pulled, the fabric's tight,
I wear my blunders with delight.
Stumbles stitched in bright array,
Patterns of a funny day.

Time's Tattered Quilt

A patch of jokes, a swatch of glee,
Each square a tale, oh can't you see?
I wear my stories to the park,
With laughter we ignite the spark.

Frayed edges speak of silly schemes,
Dancing in our wildest dreams.
A quilt of quirks in vibrant hues,
Where laughter's warmth will chase the blues.

Echoing Moments

Echoes bounce with cheeky flair,
A slip, a trip, we float in air.
Whispers giggle, break the mold,
Forgotten tales, forever told.

Each moment rings with joyous sound,
As comical mishaps come around.
Echoes blend and twist and sway,
In a funny ballet we play.

Tides of Fleeting Days

Waves of whimsy crash ashore,
With every tick, we crave for more.
Riding highs and lows with glee,
A surf of laughter, just you and me.

The sandcastle dreams that wash away,
Are just a mirthful game we play.
Each fleeting tide, a giggling spree,
Time dances by so merrily.

The Fabric of Dreams

In a world where socks might roam,
And wishes dance like bees to foam.
Every thread is tangled fun,
Weaving laughter, never done.

The pillow fights on windy nights,
Chasing giggles in playful flights.
Hypnotized by drowsy schemes,
We stitch our joy into the seams.

Rewind the Loom

Oh, how I wish to twist and twirl,
Fast-forward life, what a whirl!
But every fray and knot I see,
Is just the way life ticks for me.

Like yarn rolls competing in a race,
Each twist reveals a silly face.
Let's rewind the moments past,
With laughter's echo, we'll have a blast.

Knots of Existence

Life's a yarn in tangled threads,
A comedy where humor spreads.
We tie ourselves in silly bows,
And dance around like wiggly toes.

Each knot a tale that makes us grin,
A fabric where the fun begins.
Pull one loose, and watch it roll,
Embrace the chaos, that's the goal!

Patterns of Reflection

In mirrors where the quirks collide,
Reflections giggle, take a ride.
The patterns shift in playful flux,
We laugh at what our view constructs.

A loop-de-loop of memories sweet,
Where silly echoes come to greet.
We dance through life with threads awry,
Creating joy, oh me, oh my!

Chasing Fleeting Shadows

In the land where shadows play,
We chase them down, both night and day.
They giggle, twist, and take to flight,
Always just beyond our sight.

With a hop and skip, we zoom around,
In search of echoes that won't be found.
They tease us near, then vanish away,
As laughter lingers, brightening the gray.

Moments Woven with Care

In the fabric of the hours, we sew,
Stitching laughter, patching woe.
Each thread is golden, but some are frayed,
Crafting joy with every trade.

Silly patterns form and twist,
Moments missed but not dismissed.
We dance on threads that stretch and bend,
Life's a tapestry, round every bend.

Pendulum Dreams

Back and forth, the pendulum swings,
Tickling thoughts like fanciful wings.
Watch it dance with a wink and grin,
Time's a jester, dear, let's begin!

One moment we're wise, the next we're not,
Caught in webs that fate forgot.
We giggle as the hours zoom,
In a comical, chaotic room.

Spools of Memory

Winding tales on spools so bright,
Threads of laughter, morning light.
With every pull, a giggle flows,
Memory's dance in silly clothes.

Catch a stitch before it runs,
Life's a game of jest and puns.
Each memory spool spins a tale,
In the breeze where laughter sails.

Whispers of Yesterday

In the attic, dust bunnies dance,
Old photos giggle at their chance.
Grandma's wigs swing with flair,
Timeless stories fill the air.

Time's a jester, quite the trick,
With mismatched socks and a funny tick.
Each laugh line maps a tale,
Of shoes too big and a silly fail.

The Intricate Weft

Threads unravel, oh what a sight,
Spools of chaos throwing a fright.
Patterns jump like frogs in glee,
Knots hide secrets, come peek and see.

A stitch gone rogue, what a mess!
Fabric giggles, nothing less.
Colors clash in joyful spree,
As needles dance in wild decree.

Fragments on the Wheel

Spinning yarns in a whirlwind rhyme,
Fleecy clouds, they laugh at time.
Oops! There goes the cat again,
Attacking wool like it's a friend.

The wheel spins out tales untold,
Of knitted hats and socks so bold.
Each twist a chuckle, each turn a grin,
As laughter weaves the fun within.

Eternal Embroidery

Stitches smile, what a grand show,
Patchwork tales in every row.
Hopscotch fabric, skipping along,
With every swipe, it hums a song.

Needles jump with a playful wink,
Creating patterns faster than you think.
In the fabric of life, we find the fun,
Silly shapes and puns on the run.

The Dance of Memory

In a closet, old shoes hide,
Waiting for dances side by side.
They twirl with shadows on the floor,
Laughing at moments, wanting more.

Tickling thoughts of days gone by,
With hiccuping giggles, we can't deny.
Each step, a mishap, but oh so fun,
Chasing the echoes, one by one.

Carved into Time

A chair on the porch, creaks with glee,
Sipping lemonade, just you and me.
Memories etched like silly jokes,
Stuck in our minds like stubborn spokes.

The squirrels plot with wily schemes,
While we chuckle, sharing dreams.
Each wrinkle adds a punchline's charm,
Life's a sketchbook, always warm.

Interwoven Paths

Two paths crossed like tangled hair,
Funny how life can be unfair.
Stumbling forward, we trip on fate,
We laugh it off, it's never too late.

With silly hats and wobbly shoes,
We dance through life with quirky cues.
Each blunder adds a colorful thread,
In this fabric, no room for dread.

A Weave of Tomorrow

Threads of laughter stitch the day,
In a tapestry, bright and gay.
Each whimsy woven, kooky and light,
Making futures out of silly sights.

The sun winks with a cheeky grin,
As we chase the moments, let the fun begin.
Tomorrow's a riddle wrapped in jest,
So let's laugh wildly, forget the rest.

The Interlaced Hours

Tick-tock goes the clock,
Each hour like a sock.
Worn once then tossed away,
Just to start another day.

Days twist and twirl,
In a dizzying whirl.
Can't find the missing shoe,
While I chase my dreams anew.

Calendars flip like pancakes,
Promises turn to heartaches.
Time's a prankster, oh so sly,
Laughs as seconds pass us by.

In the quilt of our fate,
We stitch and speculate.
Every moment knits a grin,
What a quirky game we're in!

Hues of the Past

Sunset glows with orange hues,
Reminders of old, worn shoes.
Each color is a memory,
In a box, they laugh with glee.

Pinks remind me of sweet pies,
Cheerful cakes, and silly cries.
Photos fade, yet laughs remain,
Who knew we could be so insane?

Back to where the laughter grew,
Where pranks brewed like morning dew.
Spilling milk and wearing stains,
Oh, the joys, oh, the pains!

The rainbow of our youthful schemes,
Dancing in our crazy dreams.
In colors bright, we spin around,
Finding joy where lost is found.

Threads of Transience

A thread unspools, watch it glide,
Winding up on a rollercoaster ride.
Time's fabric wears and frays,
In whimsical, absurd displays.

Stitches break in the funny seams,
Trust the paths of wild dreams.
Oh, the stitches, oh, the snags,
Life's a mix of jests and rags.

We weave our tales with chuckles bright,
Knots that squeak and dance in night.
With every twist, a laughter springs,
In the tapestry of what life brings.

Unraveling threads, we laugh and cheer,
Making silly puns, that's the idea here.
Life's a patchwork, a silly jest,
In each snag, we find our zest!

Chronicles in Fabric

In the land where snippets reign,
Each fabric tells a tale insane.
Cotton clouds and velvet dreams,
Unraveling, it giggles and beams.

Chronicles of yesteryear,
We stitch together, what a cheer!
Patchwork of odd little events,
Life's great quilt, it seems, presents.

Buttons pop, zippers cling,
In the chaos, we start to sing.
A narrative woven with quips and tricks,
Magic moments in fabric mix.

Fabrics whisper, tales unfold,
Stories of the brave and bold.
In the shears of time's swift tale,
We weave a giggle, never pale.

Ghosts of Time's Gentle Hand

In the attic where old boots roam,
Ghosts are trying to find a home.
They flip through calendars on the wall,
And find last Tuesday's pizza call.

Tick-tock clocks just spin around,
While each lost sock starts to hound.
They dance like shadows, come what may,
And laugh at how they made us sway.

Old photos grin with crooked smiles,
Reminding us of our goofy styles.
But as they hover, what's their plan?
To haunt our snacks and steal our cans?

Yet laughter echoes through the years,
As we embrace our silly fears.
With ghosts of moments yet to see,
We'll dance together, you and me.

The Great Tangle of Life's Journey.

Life's a kite caught in the breeze,
Tangled strings won't put us at ease.
Each mishap makes us spin and twirl,
As we face-planted in life's whirl.

There's a little voice that loves to tease,
"Did you really think life would please?"
With every knot, we laugh and bumble,
Finding joy in each little stumble.

Maps are made of coffee stains,
Where we noted all our strains.
We'll trip along this winding way,
With smiles that light up every day.

So here's to all the twists and turns,
Where humor in each misstep burns.
Though life's a ride, we'll hang on tight,
With laughter guiding us at every height.

Threads of Eternity

Spools unfurl in a playful dance,
Each thread a tale, a silly chance.
Wrap it here, then let it go,
A fabric woven from a show.

Stitching moments, odd and grand,
With mismatched colors, slapdash planned.
It's a patchwork quilt that makes us grin,
With goofy patterns to pull us in.

In the loom of time, we loop and weave,
Every giggle something to believe.
Each snag a chance to tie a knot,
Life's a ride, believe it or not!

So let's embrace this tangled spree,
With each lost thread, we still feel free.
For in this fabric, bright and bold,
Our laughter echoes, stories told.

Frayed Minutes

Seconds slip by like a zany prank,
Frayed minutes lost at the coffee tank.
We sip and spill, we swirl and dream,
Each little mishap a perfect scheme.

Time is a dog with a wobbly tail,
Chasing its shadow, leaving a trail.
It trips over ice, does backflips too,
A hilarious sight just for me and you.

Calendars crinkle, oh what a sight,
With doodles and puns wrapped up tight.
We scribble the hours with playful hands,
Laughing at time as it whimsically stands.

So let's embrace those quirky bends,
Laughing together as time descends.
For in this mess we find delight,
Frayed minutes spinning through day and night.

The Fabric of Life's Passage

In the cupboard of life, I found some thread,
A tangled old spool, much like my head.
With every stitch, I tried to be neat,
But ended up losing my downy seat.

Time's a tailor, so cheeky and sly,
It snips and it clips as the days go by.
I wondered aloud as I struggled to sew,
Is it me or the fabric that's starting to grow?

Tangles of Fleeting Days

I once had a calendar, well-organized,
But then it got messy, I was so surprised.
Mismatched events like socks in a drawer,
My plans ran away, like kids from the store.

The clock's hands are playful, they flick and they tease,
They dance all around like a swarm of bees.
Yet here I am laughing, a clown in the scene,
Chasing my deadlines like they're painted in green.

Seamless into Forever

In a world made of stitches, I fumble and trip,
With seams that are crooked on this wild trip.
I asked for a moment, just one tiny break,
But time laughed and whispered, 'Get out for my sake!'

Eternity's fabric stretches and twirls,
While I'm stuck in a knot, like lost little pearls.
But wait! There's a mirror, oh what a delight,
I'm grooving with shadows, who knew I could bite?

Weaving Through Forgotten Paths

I wandered through threads of memories thick,
Finding old patterns that made me feel sick.
With each step I took, a tickle of fun,
Just like stepping on gum; oh what have I done?

The past is a quilt of odd shapes and hues,
Full of mismatched stories and tangled-up blues.
Yet laughter erupts when I see my reflection,
Life's just a loop in this crazy connection.

Time's Farewell Stitches

Threads of laughter in the air,
Stitches pulling at my hair.
Time's fabric wears a goofy grin,
Stitching memories, let the fun begin!

A sock with holes, a tale it tells,
Of clumsy dances and fallen spells.
Each button lost, a moment shared,
Time's quilt is wild, but we're not scared!

Echoes in the Twine

Echoes bounce like a rubber ball,
Twisting threads that never fall.
Weaving giggles into the night,
As memories dance in the pale moonlight.

Twine turned silly, a knot in time,
Riddled with punchlines, oh so sublime!
Each twist and turn, a punchy phrase,
Life's a jester, in so many ways!

The Woven Past

Woven stories, what a sight,
Crafted laughs in morning light.
The fabric frays, yet holds so tight,
A patchwork life, oh what a flight!

Through all the seams, we lose and find,
A comic strip that's well-defined.
Stitching joy into each day,
With threads of laughter all the way!

Memory's Silken Threads

Silken threads of bright review,
Tickle trunks of cotton blue.
Every knot, a laugh entwined,
In the fabric of the mind.

Seams of joy, a tailored jest,
Woven tight, we're truly blessed.
With snickers sewn and giggles spun,
Life's a quilt; we've just begun!

Memories on a String

A sock once lost, now a loyal friend,
In the dryer's whirl, where mysteries blend.
Each sneeze sets off a cosmic dance,
Who knew laundry could set dreams askance?

A jellybean fell, a taste much too bold,
Found it weeks later, a relic of old.
Now it's in the jar, a worn-out clue,
Colorful history, no longer chew!

The Warp of Existence

A cat in a box, a gift of delight,
Paws in the air, oh what a sight!
He dreams of the world, while I sip my tea,
This fluffy philosopher, oh, so carefree.

Baking a cake, I forgot all the eggs,
Turned out a brick, with some wobble and kegs.
Laughter erupts as we try to consume,
While that cake sits there, a marvel of gloom.

Layers of Yesterday

Old photos stack on a wobbly shelf,
What's that hairdo? I barely recognize myself.
Hiding back stories of outfits and friends,
Each click a reminder of trends with no ends.

An expired coupon, from ages ago,
To save fifty cents, was the star of the show.
But in distant memories, it proudly resides,
In the chaos of time, it never quite hides.

Shadows in the Fabric

A sock puppet show, for an empty chair,
Dramatic choruses fill the air.
We laugh at the plots, so silly and bright,
As the puppets scheme under fluorescent light.

A sneeze from the couch, sends cats on the run,
Their wild acrobatics, oh, so much fun!
Yesterday's chaos, in shadows now play,
A tapestry woven in laughter today.

Fragments of a Woven Journey

Threads of everyday mischief,
Knotted tales in a rush.
A sock goes missing, oh dear,
It's hidden in the lunch!

Laughs from old granddad's chair,
Spinning yarns of the past.
Each snip and poke a memory,
In stitches made to last.

The Tapestry of Hours

With every tick, a giggle,
The clock dances on the wall.
Minutes doing the cha-cha,
While seconds trip and fall.

Coffee spills like clock hands,
A blend of chaos brewed.
But in this mess of my mornings,
A joyful mood is mooded.

Hues of Fleeting Shadows

Colors blend and swirl around,
Caught in a playful chase.
Shadows wink and hide away,
Leaving behind a trace.

A dance of beams and giggles,
On walls where laughter plays.
Each hue, a mischief-maker,
In the light of sunny days.

Strings of Yesterday's Dreams

Tangled themes of what once was,
Like noodles on a plate.
Twists and turns in slumber's grip,
Oh, what a funny fate!

Chasing dreams with silly hats,
In fields where daisies grow.
Every laugh a little thread,
In the fabric of our flow.

Shimmering Threads of the Past

In the cupboard, memories hide,
Like socks that no one can find.
Each thread a tale, each string a joke,
We laugh at the past as it strokes our cloak.

Grandma's stories, tangled and neat,
Of dancing cats on twinkle toes fleet.
We'll spin them round, we'll spin them again,
Into a yarn with a playful spin!

Bobby pins, lost in a sea of hair,
How many times has that caused despair?
Yet every mishap, a giggle or two,
As we thread nostalgia with a quirky view.

From childhood games, to socks with holes,
Life is a quilt that humor consoles.
Let's sew those moments with laughter anew,
In the fabric of time, let's bid adieu.

The Dance of Infinite Echoes

Echoes bounce like a rubber ball,
Whispering stories that never fall.
They trip on toes, then giggle away,
In the dance hall of memories, we sway.

Chasing laughter that swims like fish,
Each ripple a sweet, forgotten wish.
We waltz through blunders with shuffling feet,
As echoes of silly make our night complete.

Tickling fancies from days gone by,
With every twirl, we can't help but sigh.
When time was a clown with a painted nose,
We danced to the rhythm of our own doze.

So grab a partner, lend them a cheer,
Let's swirl through the past, with smiles sincere.
In this echo dance, with whimsy and glee,
We'll laugh through the ages, just you and me.

Moments Caught in the Weave

Moments caught in an endless thread,
Like pancakes flipped, some fell on their head!
Every moment, a flavor to taste,
A smorgasbord of life, no time to waste!

Spinning tales on a windy day,
Where kites are tangled in their own ballet.
Each gust a giggle, each flutter a plea,
For a moment of freedom, oh let it be free!

The loom of laughter links hearts like glue,
Binding us tighter with every 'boo-hoo.'
In stitches of mirth, we weave quite the thread,
To snuggle in joy, and banish the dread.

So gather your quirks, your mishaps and fun,
Each moment of folly, let's roll out as one.
In this fabric of life, let's dance and weep,
With threads of laughter, our memories keep.

Fading Colors of a Distant Echo

Fading colors in a tapestry bright,
Remind us of laughter that took flight.
Like crayons left out in the summer sun,
They remind us of silly games we've spun.

Echoes of giggles, like whispers in space,
Floating on breezes, a playful embrace.
Each hue a jest, from wild to the tame,
In this portrait of time, we're all part of the game.

The shades of our folly, they lighten the gloom,
As we paint with the blush of an old dusty broom.
Let's dance in the fading, let's laugh at the past,
For every echo, a moment to cast.

So gather your colors, bright palette or grey,
Let's tiptoe through memories, come what may.
In this fading delight, let's capture the glow,
With laughter as our guide, we'll explore and bestow.

The Cord of Existence

Life's a string, we tug and pull,
Like a cat that's found a spool.
Every laugh, a loop we make,
In silly dances, we all shake.

Moments twist, then untwist fast,
As we trip over jokes that last.
Bouncing from one detail to the next,
Our cord's a mix of funny text.

Reflections in the Fabric

In mirrors framed by silly threads,
We spot the clothes our humor bled.
Patchwork joys, mismatched delight,
Like socks that vanish out of sight.

Laughter shows in every seam,
Life's a quilt of goofy dreams.
With every stitch, we find our glee,
In patterned chaos, wild and free.

Knots in the Journey

Tangled paths we wander through,
With shoelaces tied in knots anew.
Each hiccup gives us tales to share,
Like how I tripped and lost my hair.

Around the bends, we juggle fate,
With goofy grins and lots of plate.
Losing socks along the ride,
In laughter's arms, we all abide.

Weaving With Time

In a loom of laughter, we entwine,
Mismatched days, a wobbly line.
Every second's a loop undone,
With hiccups loud, we've barely won.

Spinning yarns of silly grace,
Chasing time, it's quite the race.
Threads of joy, we weave them bright,
In this fabric, life's a flight.

The Woven Echo

In a fabric shop, I lost my thread,
Caught in stitches that danced instead.
Each pattern whispered a silly tease,
Yet I tangled with laughter, if you please.

With bobbins rolling all over the floor,
I tripped on yarn, then found some more.
A needle's wink, a spool's sly grin,
Sewing joy was where I'd begin.

Tapestries laughed in wild array,
They spun around in a colorful ballet.
Every loop a chuckle, every knot a cheer,
In this mad weave, I shouted, "I'm here!"

As I stitched my way through fabric so fine,
Each thread of joy becoming divine.
With each weird twist and every new blend,
I discovered that laughs are the best kind of mend.

The Rich Cloth of Dreams

In dreams I walk on threads of gold,
Sewing stories yet untold.
A patchwork quilt of goofy sights,
Where penguins dance on neon nights.

Buttons pop and zippers sing,
As I stitch my way through tiny bling.
Each fabric choice—oh what a mess!
Yet laughter hides in every stress.

Patterns clash like cats and dogs,
While my fabric morphs to hungry frogs.
A quilt of quirks like no other seam,
In my world of dreams, it's all a meme.

So gather your threads and bring your threadbare,
Let's sew up giggles beyond compare.
Wrap me in this silly, plush embrace,
In a tapestry where laughter finds its place.

Tangles of Twilight

Twilight approaches, oh what a sight,
As strings of yarn take to flight.
They twist and twirl with playful glee,
Chasing shadows just like me.

A loop-de-loop around my feet,
I tumble and roll, it's quite the treat.
A shawl of giggles wrapped around,
In this twilight fun, happiness is found.

Every strand a joke untold,
In a fabric maze that dares be bold.
I weave through chuckles, stitch by stitch,
In a twilight jig, I find my niche.

As day bows down and night draws near,
I embrace the tangled threads with cheer.
So let's knit mischief, let's cut the gloom,
In this fabric dance, let laughter bloom.

The Fiber of Experience

Threads of life weave wild and strange,
With every twist, there's always a change.
A spool of mishaps, a needle of fate,
In my tapestry, it's never too late.

Oh, the fibers tell tales with a humorous bend,
Each stitch in the fabric is destined to blend.
From slipping and sliding in clumsy delight,
To laughing at yarns that keep me up at night.

Journeying through fuzz and vibrant hues,
My experience grows, as do the blues.
Knots of folly, I embrace their call,
In this woven life, I stitch it all.

Let's thread our laughter through every seam,
Creating a quilt from the silliest dream.
So gather your fibers, let's wear them bold,
In this fabric of life, let our stories be told.

A Stitch in the Present

Time's a quirky little beast,
Stitching patterns on our feast.
Wobbly threads in a hurry,
Let's laugh at this grand flurry.

Each moment's got a punchline,
A tickle in the grand design.
Sewing memories that won't fade,
In mismatched socks, we've got it made.

So grab your needle, and let's weave,
A tapestry none would believe.
With laughter as our silent seam,
We'll hold together this silly dream.

The Pendulum's Embrace

A pendulum swings with quite a flair,
Tick-tock jokes, hanging in midair.
Sometimes it laughs, sometimes it cries,
Wobbling truths in a world of lies.

Round and round it goes, oh my!
Watch it dance and flutter by.
Each sway a tale with a quirky view,
Like socks that mysteriously grew.

Embracing moments with grace and glee,
Finding joy in the absurdity.
So let it swing, let it sway,
With chuckles that brighten the grey.

Threads of Lost Journeys

Threads of journeys unwind and twist,
We miss our train, but who needs the mist?
Maps that lead us to hilarious ends,
Where ducks wear hats, and humor bends.

Lost in laughs, we wander wide,
Finding treasures with each stride.
A compass that points to silly things,
Like dancing rocks and grammar kings.

Though routes may shift like jello on fire,
We chase those moments that never tire.
So come take a trip, join the ride,
Where laughter waits and time won't hide.

Fragments of Fate

Fragments of fate, precarious and bright,
Scatter like confetti, wild in flight.
With every slip, a giggle escapes,
As fate trips over its own capes.

Each piece a joke in a puzzle unclear,
Shaped by chuckles and the odd sneer.
Banana peels on the path we tread,
Witty whispers from the paper shred.

So gather those bits, let's craft a plan,
With laughter as our lucky span.
In the tapestry of what we've braced,
Humor is the stitch that's laced.

The Passage Between

In a world where socks go to hide,
The gap between minutes is wide.
A tick-tock echo through the hall,
Chasing my shadow, I feel so small.

The cat's got a plan, oh, what a fiend,
Stretched on the sofa, he's living the dream.
While I rush for time, he's perfectly fine,
In the game of life, he wins every dime.

My coffee's gone cold, my hair's a fright,
Who knew that brunch could last till night?
A calendar full, but I can't keep score,
With each passing tick, I just want more.

So here's to the moments that slip and slide,
Where laughter and chaos tend to reside.
In this dance of days, I'll join the spree,
And laugh at the clock, both wild and free.

Spinning Memories

Round and round like a merry-go-round,
The moments stack up without a sound.
A wink from the past, a nod from today,
I trip over memories in the fray.

Jellybeans in pockets, a spritz of cologne,
A dance in the kitchen, we're never alone.
The clock slaps my wrist, a comedic jest,
"Your time is up!"—what a pointless quest!

Cartwheels in summer, slips in the frost,
With each joyful laugh, the present is lost.
But up comes a giggle, a tickle, a squawk,
As I blush and remember the time on the clock.

Here's to the spinning of tales so fine,
With giggles and grins that warp and entwine.
A tapestry woven from moments so bold,
In this funny old life, they never grow old.

Relics of the Clock

Dusty clocks grinning with goofy glee,
Yet they tick-tock silently, just like me.
With cogs that laugh and hands that dance,
Time shows no mercy, no second glance.

Gather up knickknacks from days gone by,
A rubber duck, a bad tie, oh my!
Each relic a footstep, a puzzle piece,
In this jester's journey, let's just laugh and cease.

Tick-tock goes the hour while I sing a tune,
Waiting for constellations, or maybe a moon.
The universe chuckles, as I trip on a shoe,
With memories amusing, too many to view.

Old calendars whisper of yesterdays lost,
But laughter's the currency—what's the cost?
To dance with the moments we cherish and share,
Is the sweetest of treasures, with time to spare.

Captured Seconds

They say seconds are fleeting, but mine just arrived,
With hiccups and giggles, they prance and they dive.
A pocketful of nonsense, a sprinkle of cheer,
Captured in snapshots, from far to near.

Jumping in puddles, with rubbery glee,
Counting the giggles, it's just you and me.
Time twists and tangles, like yarn on the floor,
As we chase after laughter, who could ask for more?

With twirls and a spin, our worries take flight,
As we catch up with moments late into the night.
The world spins in circles, a grand carousel,
Each second a story, each laugh a spell.

So here's to our chronicle, quirky and bright,
A patchwork of happiness, day and night.
In this raucous riot, let's never be tame,
Captured are seconds—oh what a game!

Tangled Narratives

Once I met a clock with a grin,
It giggled and spun, let the chaos begin.
Tick-tock it would dance, making quite the fuss,
Turning minutes to noodles, oh what a plus!

A jester named Time wore mismatched shoes,
Lost all his purpose, ran out of clues.
He juggled my past, tossed memories high,
Then tripped on a moment and watched it fly!

In a world made of yarn, I knitted and knotted,
With every stitch, another truth plotted.
Peeking in corners, where shadows had bled,
I found all my secrets, now tangled in thread.

So here we are now, in this funny old tale,
With clocks that are laughing and winds that set sail.
Let's dance to the rhythm, of a frivolous rhyme,
Life's best in the chaos, a beautiful mime!

Hand-Sewn Histories

Old tales sewn up with colorful threads,
Quilting the past where the humor spreads.
Each patch tells a story, both silly and bright,
Like granddad's mustache that took quite a bite!

There's a button from Paris, a zipper from Spain,
A pocket of nonsense, a buttoned-up train.
Each seam carries laughter, a joke or a pun,
As we braid our adventures, all under the sun.

Stitched memories flutter like flags in the breeze,
Every knot a reminder, life's quirky tease.
With each funny stitch, we craft and we weave,
A tapestry spun from the days we believe.

So gather your scraps and let's make a scene,
With laughter and joy, we'll create a machine!
Hand-sewn histories tickle the mind,
In this wacky old world, it's giggles we find!

Threads of Nostalgia

Picture a sweater, frayed at the seams,
Each thread holds a memory, or so it seems.
Worn by a dreamer who danced in the rain,
Claiming each droplet was never in vain.

A cat on a pillow, a dog with a sock,
Time's funny game with a tick and a tock.
Like gravy on biscuits, or jelly on toast,
These threads of nostalgia, we cherish the most.

But what if a napkin became a bouquet?
What if our pasts all decided to play?
They'd twirl and they'd tumble, so carefree and light,
In the fabric of memory, they'd take endless flight.

So, gather your threads, let nostalgia ignite,
In a quilt of our laughter, everything feels right.
Each stitch full of giggles, and every line pure gold,
Life's comical fabric, forever unfolds!

Fading Imprints

In a land where the footprints of laughter remain,
Fading imprints whisper jokes in the rain.
Each step tells a tale, a prank or a jest,
Leaving behind echoes of moments, the best.

With shadows that giggle and breezes that tease,
Fading imprints hold secrets, like light through the trees.
A leap off the sidewalk, a hop by the gate,
Each mischief we ventured, oh wasn't it great!

A puddle reflects all our slip-ups with glee,
As we chase after giggles that flutter like bees.
The path zigzags forward, we trip and we slide,
In those hilarious moments, we learn how to glide.

So here's to the footprints, both faded and bold,
In the playful embrace of the stories we've told.
With every soft giggle, every stomp and a dance,
Fading imprints remind us, life's one big chance!

The Fabric of What Was

In the closet of the past, I found,
A sweater knitted with laughter all around.
But each time I wore it, it shrank a bit,
Now it fits my cat, isn't that a hit?

A sock with holes, a tragic plight,
It looked so grand in the morning light.
Now it dances in the dryer's spin,
Where lost socks win, and mischiefs begin!

Each button tells tales of meals gone wrong,
The stains are stories in a fabric song.
The seams are secrets that whisper and sigh,
But sewing mishaps still make me laugh and try!

So here's to fabric, its quirks and twists,
Time may try, but it can't resist.
For every thread that comes undone,
A funny memory, stitched just for fun!

Stitches of Remembrance

Caught in a loop of a knitting spree,
My scarf turned into a woolen tree.
It tangled my feet during a winter ball,
I guess fashion's humor is always a thrill!

Each stitch a moment that didn't comply,
Like that time I tried eating cake, oh my!
The fluff went flying, and so did my plan,
Now I'm known as the frosting fan!

Remember the shirt with a pocket so grand,
But only for change, not for hand?
I lost my phone and can't find my way,
Each stitch a reminder of my clumsy play.

Ah, the knitted memories, the perfectly wrong,
They wrap me in laughter, a comical song.
With fabric and thread, I'll weave through the night,
In stitches of joy, everything feels right!

Threads Unraveled

Once I attempted a grand crochet,
But the yarn went wild, like a beast at play.
It roamed the room, a colorful spree,
Till it tripped my dog, oh, what a sight to see!

My sweater was once a perfect fit,
Now it resembles a potato, I'll admit.
With sleeves that dangle and a neck so wide,
I'm still the trendsetter in this fabric tide!

The button jar is a time capsule for sure,
With mismatched pairs that often endure.
Like friends at parties who don't quite align,
Together they laugh, it's a comical sign!

So as I weave through these tangled days,
I find the humor in the fabric maze.
Every unraveled thread could lead to a laugh,
In this dance of mischief, I'm the perfect half!

Dance of the Seconds

A clock on the wall strikes an hour so sly,
While the seconds just giggle as they rush by.
I tried to dance to their frantic beat,
But tripped on my tongue, now isn't that sweet?

With each minute that passes by fast,
I ponder how fun times never last.
Yet here I am, on my wobbly legs,
Doing the cha-cha with some curious pegs!

Each tick-tock's a joke that time likes to tell,
In a moment of laughter, and oh, so well.
I twirl through mishaps, my spirits fly high,
In this goofy rumble, I touch the sky!

So let's celebrate time, a whimsical friend,
With every faux pas, there's joy to lend.
In the dance of seconds, we sway and we spin,
No doubt about it, let the fun times begin!

Elusive Moments

I chased a squirrel up a tree,
It laughed and mocked right back at me.
A flash of fur, a nut then lost,
In this grand race, I'm not the boss.

A sock I lost, it took a trip,
Was it the dryer or the ship?
I'll never know, but here's the clue:
Socks have a life; they're wild and flew.

The clock strikes loud, I jump in fright,
Was it the dinner or the light?
I find the food with much delight,
But all too soon, it's out of sight.

So here I stand, a fool at play,
With fleeting joys that slip away.
In every laugh, a lesson's song,
Time spins around; it won't be long.

Veils of the Infinite

The cat prefers to nap all day,
As if the world's a silly play.
While I attempt to clean the floor,
She blinks and yawns, I hear her snore.

I bought a plant that's quite the star,
It drooped and wilted, then went far.
Was it the light or lack of care?
It seems my skills are quite a scare.

The coffee pot went for a swim,
In a suitcase made for dry whim.
I brewed a mess of joy and cream,
And woke to find it was a dream.

Here's to the things that slip away,
Like socks, like dreams, like yesterday.
We laugh and dance in every blunder,
For life's a joke, a peaceful thunder.

Echoes in the Weave

A bird sang loud, then lost its voice,
It dropped a note, it had no choice.
I tried to catch it, gently weep,
But feathers flew, it's time to sleep.

I spilled my drink—what a delight!
It looked like art, quite a sight!
All the colors blend and rave,
Yet my shirt cannot be saved.

In every blink, a tale unfolds,
Like yarn unraveling from old molds.
I chase the threads, they twist and dive,
But giggling hearts keep dreams alive.

With every laugh, a stitch in time,
We weave our woes to silly rhyme.
In every error, joy ignites,
Echoes of laughter, pure highlights.

Frayed Dreams

I tried to bake a cake so grand,
But flour drifted from my hand.
It danced around like it was free,
My kitchen turned into a spree.

The mirror laughed when I walked by,
Who is that? Oh me, oh my!
It seems my hair has lost the fight,
A goofy crown, a funny sight.

I thought I'd run a quick errand,
But tripped on roots, I felt a tear-and-
With grapes that rolled and milk that flew,
The grocery list turned into brew.

Yet in this mess of frayed delight,
I find the joy, the funny bite.
For every search that takes a turn,
In life's grand joke, there's always learn.

The Interlaced Stories of Us

In a sock drawer, secrets hide,
Lost left shoes, their stories bide.
Once a dance, now a game of fate,
With each mismatch, we celebrate!

Fuzzy sweaters from long ago,
Tales of laughter, laughter in tow.
Coffee stains and crumbs delight,
Moments woven, oh what a sight!

Jumbled thoughts on napkins lay,
Doodles that paved our silly way.
We slip and slide through days of cheer,
As memories knit, we hold them near!

So let us spin these tales aloud,
Of all the times we felt so proud.
In tangled knots, our lives entwine,
These quirky threads, forever shine!

Woven Memories of Wandering

A map discarded, off we roam,
Lost in laughter, finding home.
Ice cream spills and giggles rise,
Chasing sunsets in the skies.

Sand between our toes, we race,
Seagulls swoop, a comical chase.
With each wrong turn, a new delight,
Our woven tales soar to new heights!

From parks to streets with balloon rides,
Each winding path, our joy abides.
We flip the script, the world our stage,
In this grand play, we turn the page!

So wander on, my friend so dear,
With moments spun, let's persevere.
For every trip, a giggle's due,
In woven threads, it's me and you!

Chronicles Beneath the Surface

Underneath the bed, what lies?
Dust bunnies crafting their own guise.
Whispers of toys from days so bright,
Conversations held deep in the night.

Old board games with missing dice,
Wagers made and once in a vice.
Cards and snacks, we compete with glee,
In these chronicles, we're truly free!

A treasure trove of lost remotes,
Stories of shows and wild anecdotes.
Each click unfolds a laugh or two,
In the shadows, our fun's peek-a-boo!

So lift the rug, uncover the past,
These chronicles of ours will last.
What's hidden deep, let's also find,
With chortles echoing, hearts aligned!

Reflections in the Weft of Being

Mirrored faces, silly grins,
Each reflection, where life begins.
Splashing through puddles, we broadly beam,
In this light, we laugh and dream!

Quirky hats and mismatched socks,
In the mirror, each giggle knocks.
With every glance, we find our glee,
Embracing quirks, like birds in a tree.

We dance like no one's watching near,
With every twirl, we shed a tear.
Twirling round, the world's our joy,
In this reflection, every girl and boy!

So look again, at all you see,
In weft of being, wild and free.
Each moment sparkles, lights our way,
In laughter's bloom, forever stay!

Threads of Moments

In the garden of socks, funny threads unwind,
Silly stories woven, in chaos we find.
A fashion faux pas, a hat on a cat,
With laughter and giggles, we tiptoe and chat.

Time wears a bowtie, its colors are bright,
Jumps into jello, a slippery sight.
Bananas wear helmets, they dance on the floor,
Life's a circus act; who could ask for more?

The clock plays a tune, it's wobbly and wild,
It skips like a kid, it's forever beguiled.
Round and round we spin, on a merry-go-round,
A carousel of quirks, in laughter we're found.

With each silly tick, the day's punchline grows,
We gather our joy, wear it like our clothes.
In this whimsical ride, we twist and we twine,
For moments are threads, and they're all yours and mine.

Frayed Edges of Memory

A chicken in pajamas, that's how we roll,
Memory's frayed edge, with a tickle and troll.
A dance at the fridge, a trip over shoes,
In the land of the quirky, we're never to lose.

Silly hats on our heads, so mismatched and bright,
Echoes of laughter, they dance in the light.
With each coffee spill, comes a new joke to tell,
Frayed edges of memory, oh, can't you tell?

A pickle in the pocket, a cat with a shoe,
These moments, they linger, in shades of the new.
Each hiccup a giggle, a slip and a slide,
In the scrapbook of life, humor's our guide.

We laugh through the ages, a blur in the frame,
With every misstep, we relish the game.
So here's to the quirky, the frayed and the fun,
In the tapestry woven, we're never quite done.

Whispers of Yesteryears

Socks talk in whispers, in corners they scheme,
Gathering memories, like a sweet little dream.
Dancing in slippers, with laughter we twirl,
In the ballet of blunders, we find our own pearl.

The past wears a smile, so crooked and wide,
With echoes of pranks, it's a jolly old ride.
A toaster that speaks, with a buttery grin,
Reminds us that laughter is where we begin.

With jumpy old toys, we bumble and bounce,
Every tickle and poke, a gleeful announce.
In snippets of stories, we belly-ache roar,
Each whisper of yesteryears asks for more.

So here's to the antics, the laughs that we share,
The giggles that twinkle, as if in mid-air.
Through whispering moments, we craft our delight,
In the scrapbook of laughter, everything's right.

Echoes from the Past

In the closet of echoes, old shoes start to dance,
They riddle and wiggle, in quirky romance.
A time machine spins, with a giggle and twirl,
As we trip through the ages, all silly and swirl.

Old photos wink at us, with their mustaches wide,
Each feathered hairdo has nowhere to hide.
Pranks played with vigor, like cats on a spree,
Echoes from the past, all laughing with glee.

A bicycle chase, with a dog on the side,
In a world of mishaps, we take such great pride.
A pie in the face, what a glorious mess,
Time giggles along, in its silly excess.

So here's to the echoes, the chuckles and cheers,
The memories merry, lost under the years.
In the tapestry bright, with its colors so vast,
We savor the moments, the echoes from the past.

www.ingramcontent.com/pod-product-compliance
Lightning Source LLC
Chambersburg PA
CBHW070310120526
44590CB00017B/2608